P9-ELV-858

SCHOLASTIC'S A+ GUIDE TO BOOK REPORTS

Over a million junior high and high school students have used Scholastic's A + Guides to raise their grades, do better in every subject, and *enjoy* school more. Now you can, too!

SCHOLASTIC'S A +
GUIDE TO GOOD GRADES

SCHOLASTIC'S A +
GUIDE TO GOOD WRITING

SCHOLASTIC'S A +
GUIDE TO TAKING TESTS

SCHOLASTIC'S A +
GUIDE TO GRAMMAR

SCHOLASTIC'S A +
GUIDE TO RESEARCH AND TERM PAPERS

SCHOLASTIC'S A +
GUIDE TO BOOK REPORTS

SCHOLASTIC'S A+ GUIDE TO BOOK REPORTS

LOUISE COLLIGAN

SCHOLASTIC INC.
New York Toronto London Auckland Sydney Tokyo

No part of this publication may be reproduced in whole or in part, or stored in a retrieval system, or transmitted in any form or by any means, electronic, mechanical, photocopying, recording, or otherwise, without written permission of the publisher. For information regarding permission, write to Scholastic Inc., 730 Broadway, New York, NY 10003.

ISBN 0-590-33313-5

Copyright © 1982 by Louise Colligan. All rights reserved. Published by Scholastic Inc.

12 11 10 9 8 7 6 5 4 3 2 1   8   4 5 6 7 8/8

Printed in the U.S.A.   06

CONTENTS

To William Hogan and Teresa Foley

Chapter 1

ON YOUR MARK:
Getting Started on Your Book Report

The first semester of your English class is under way. You have kept up on most of your homework, taken a couple of quizzes, and maybe even written a composition or two. Things were going great until you got the first book report assignment of the year.

You remember the reports you did last year; they're crumpled up in the bottom drawer of your desk at home. It's all coming back to you. You spent a couple of weeks reading a pretty good book. Well, at least it was pretty good until you had to write about it. You spent a few nights writing a plot summary, and the night before the due date, you had three pages of plot and still hadn't gotten to the good stuff. But with the deadline right on top of you, you didn't really have much time to go any farther than the summary, so you kind of let things trail off, getting in one or two lines about a couple of characters. Then you wound up recommending the book, but secretly doubted that your report would encourage anybody else to read it.

Somewhere between eagerly turning the pages and writing about what happened on those pages, you lost interest in the book. Writing about it just killed your reading experience.

You got this book report guide because you would like less hassle and more fun (not to mention a better grade) the next time around. Even if those aren't your reasons, this book will show you how to pick out the most enjoyable books, how to read them productively *and* pleasurably, and how to write a report you'll be proud of.

10 STEPS TO A HASSLE-FREE BOOK REPORT

Any big job becomes more manageable when you break it down into smaller tasks. Here's how to take control of your book report assignment and work on it in a step-by-step way:

Step 1: Write down all the information about the assignment.
Step 2: Make up a schedule for writing the report.
Step 3: Plan your reading.
Step 4: Begin reading, taking notes as you do so.
Step 5: Develop a thesis statement.
Step 6: Use your notes to make up an outline.

Step 7: Write a rough draft.
Step 8: Revise and proofread your rough draft.
Step 9: Write the final draft.
Step 10: Turn your paper in on time.

There you have it—ten short steps for making a big job easier. Now let's look at what each step involves.

Step 1: Write down all the information about the assignment.

The work on your report begins before you even choose a book, on the day you get the assignment. Besides marking down the due date, there are several important questions to clear up with your teacher before you do anything else:

★ **What kind of book are you supposed to write about?** Some teachers expect you to choose titles from an assigned list. Others want you to include in your reading plans a variety of book genres or types such as fiction, nonfiction, biography, and drama. Even if your teacher leaves the choice completely up to you, find out whether you have to check back with her once you have picked out a book. Most teachers like to know ahead of time what their students are reading to make sure the reading level, subject, and theme are appropriate for a particular grade.

★ **What should you include in your report?** If your teacher hands out guidelines, make sure you understand all the requirements. While some teachers only require a plot summary, others expect a fully developed essay that covers specific aspects of the book. You'll learn all about essay-style book reports, summaries, and critiques in Chapter 3 and find hundreds of other book report topics in Chapter 4. Again, do let your teacher know what kind of report or project you plan to do if the choice is up to you. Maybe he's seen one too many clay models of the whale in *Moby Dick* or had his fill of amateur book jackets, posters, and stage sets.

★ **Are you supposed to type the report? Present it in a folder?**

★ **How long should the report be?** While a skilled and experienced writer can produce an excellent summary in less than a page, most student writers need a couple of pages to cover things like theme, plot, characterization, style, and setting. Your teacher may look askance at a report that is too short, or, on the other hand, may not want to get bogged down in a rambling account.

★ **Is there a penalty for a late paper?** You will have an extra incentive to get your report in on time if you know there's some kind of point penalty for a late one.

Make sure you get answers to all these questions in your notebook. Nothing is more frustrating than sitting down to write, only to discover that you can't remember whether you were supposed to do an analysis of the book or just a summary.

What else can you do to become a book report

whiz? Get in the habit of reading movie and book reviews in magazines like *Time, Newsweek, Seventeen, Glamour, Mademoiselle, Scope, Junior Scholastic,* and *Senior Scholastic.* In a short amount of space, professional critics write concise reviews that give readers a quick taste of a book or movie, and that should be your aim, too.

When you read published reviews, notice how they are organized. Good reviewers sum up the plot in just a few sentences, saving the greatest amount of space for discussing their views about the work. Look for the details that give you a feeling of the whole book or movie. Does the writer offer examples of the dialogue, descriptions of the settings, analyses of the style or direction? These are all elements you'll want to include in your own writing.

To learn more about what your teacher expects, see if you can track down reports other students have written. What kinds of papers got high or low marks? For your own reference, start a file of all your own tests, papers, and reports. After a while, you'll notice a pattern in your writing strengths and weaknesses, and you will know what to play up or avoid in your writing assignments.

Step 2: Make up a schedule for writing the report.

A survey of English classes would probably reveal that a high percentage of students sweat over most of their writing assignments at the very last moment. That's the nerve-wracking way to do the job. To save time you'll find that a step-by-step schedule comes in handy. Here's a model to follow:

Book Report Schedule

Due date for report: _____

Jobs to be done:	Due Date:	Completed:
1. Get assignment and know what is required.	_____	_____
2. Find at least two possible books and check them out with teacher. (Do this as soon as you get assignment.)	_____	_____
3. Start reading. (Divide number of pages by number of days before due date, allowing 4 to 5 days for writing.)	_____	_____
4. Finish book and write detailed notes.	_____	_____
5. Decide on book report topic and check it out with teacher.	_____	_____
6. Make up outline.	_____	_____
7. Write rough draft.	_____	_____
8. Proofread rough draft.	_____	_____
9. Rewrite rough draft.	_____	_____
10. Complete paper and turn it in.	_____	_____

Step 3: Plan your reading.

Reading a book for pleasure *and* for a book report assignment will coincide if you take the time to scout out good books. Talk to friends who like to read. Ask a friendly librarian for suggestions. If your teacher expects you to choose books from an assigned list, ask her to suggest a few specific titles students have really enjoyed in the past. Check the latest best-seller lists. Think about the kinds of books you have enjoyed before. The Reading Interest Quiz at the end of this chapter will help you learn more about your likes and dislikes.

You'll find a student-compiled recommended reading list in Chapter 5 of this book, along with the names of reference books that describe the kinds of reading materials that appeal to teen-agers.

Once you have half a dozen or so good suggestions, browse through the library or a book-store. Publishers spend a lot of money for copywriters who write enticing book blurbs and jacket copy to attract readers. Read the back-cover and jacket descriptions to help you narrow your choices.

What are the best sources for getting books? Your classroom, school, and town libraries are the first places to check. Or consider swapping your favorite books with a friend. You might even suggest that your teacher organize a class book swap of reading favorites. Classroom book clubs offer inexpensive paperbacks geared to your age group and interest level.

Whatever your source, choose at least two books for your assignment. Don't get stuck with a boring book just because it's too late to hunt down a better one. You could wind up writing a dull, boring report if that's how you feel about the book.

Finally, keep in mind that you can report on a book you have read already. If you spent the summer reading *Jaws*, why not write about it, if your teacher gives you the go-ahead? The reading time you save can be spent writing a terrific report.

What kind of reader are you? To help you decide what types of books are likely to appeal to you, take the following quiz:

Reading Interest Quiz

	Yes	No
1. Is Valentine's Day your favorite holiday?		✓
2. Are you a fan of "real-life" television shows, news programs, and "magazine" type programs?		✓
3. Are you intrigued by haunted houses?	✓	
4. Do you wish you could book a seat on the space shuttle?		✓
5. Do you love oddball facts and trivia?	✓	
6. Are most of your favorite songs, movies, and poems		

about love? ____ ✓

7. Do you want to improve your life, change yourself, or learn a new skill? ____ ✓

8. Do puzzles and riddles intrigue you? ✓ ____

9. Do you wonder why people fall in love? ____ ____

10. Do you believe there is intelligent life in outer space? ____ ✓

11. Are you the kind of person who's mainly interested in facts and real events? ____ ✓

12. Do you wonder what forces and events shape a person's identity? ____ ✓

13. Do you believe in UFOs? ____ ✓

14. Do you follow murder trials, heists, and the police blotter in the newspaper? ✓ ____

15. Is Halloween one of your favorite holidays? ✓ ____

16. Are you interested in seeing how people cope with personal problems? ✓ ____

17. Are your favorite movies about outer space? ____ ✓

18. Do news articles, shows, and movies about ghosts, weird animals, or haunted places grab your attention? ____ ✓

19. Do other people's lives fascinate you? ✓ ____

20. Do you wonder what makes people "tick"? ✓ ____

Here is how to score yourself:

★ If you answered *yes* more than once (questions 1, 6, or 9), you will probably enjoy reading a good love story for your next book report.

★ If you answered *yes* more than once (to questions 2, 5, 7, or 11), head for the non-fiction section of your library or bookstore, because you will probably enjoy reading oddball fact books, self-help books, or biographies.

★ If you answered *yes* more than once (to questions 3, 15, or 18), wait for the next dark and stormy night to curl up with a good ghost or horror story.

★ Your mind is in another world and time if you answered *yes* more than once (to questions 4, 10, 13, or 17). Science fiction books are your best bet.

★ You are an amateur sleuth and would probably like a good mystery if you answered *yes* to questions 8 and 14.

★ You are curious about how people behave if you answered *yes* to questions 12, 16, 19, and 20. So a novel or biography is a good choice for you. Check out young adult novels as well.

Chapter 4 is filled with a variety of book report ideas and projects to match up with books from each of these categories.

You don't believe in quizzes like these and still need help finding good books? Fill out the following survey and share the results with your teacher or librarian.

A Personal Reading Survey

1. I generally read about _____ book(s) every _____ week, __1__ month, _____ year.
2. The last two unassigned books I read were:
   ___They Led the way___ _____
   (title)   (author)
   ___John Hancock___ _____
   (title)   (author)
3. I __✓__ did _____ did not enjoy these books because ___they were about___ ___peoples lives___
4. In the last few years, two books I really enjoyed reading were ___Little Women___ ___John Hancock___
5. I wish I could find another book like _____
   (name of book)
   because _____

6. My favorite free-time activities are _____
   _____
7. Hobbies, sports, projects I enjoy most are _____
   _____
8. My favorite television programs are _____
   _____
9. My all-time favorite movies are _____
   _____
10. I like books that deal with (rank your preferences: 1 = most favorite, 2 = second most favorite, 3 = least favorite):
   _____ romance   _____ the sea
   _____ self-   _____ mythology
          improvement   science
   _____ western life   _____ future
   _____ crime and   worlds and
          mystery   outer space

11

- _____ real people's lives
- _____ politics
- _____ fantasy
- _____ adventure
- _____ history
- _____ war
- _____ family life
- _____ teenage problems
- _____ occult
- _____ oddball facts
- _____ sports
- _____ animals
- _____ spies
- _____ times and places of the past
- _____ social problems
- _____ humor
- _____ school life
- _____ other (list below)

_____

_____

Chapter 2

BOOKING IT:
Reading and Analyzing Books

Have you ever had this experience? You are partway through a book report. You remember there was a line from the book that would be perfect to include in your paper. What was it? You think it's somewhere in the last third of the book. And you are *positive* it was on the bottom right-hand side of the page. So you skim the last third of the book, searching all over for it. No luck. Half an hour later, you give up and decide you won't include the line in your report after all. Not only that, you can't remember a couple of other details you were planning to use, and it's just too time-consuming to search for them now. Instead you write your report minus the information that would have livened it up, tied all your ideas together, and probably impressed your teacher as well. So you wind up settling for a mediocre grade when you could have gotten a better one.

Here's what to do the next time around to make sure you have key bits of dialogue, descriptions, passages, and significant quotations right on hand when you start writing your report.

Step 4: Begin reading, taking notes as you do so.

Unless you have a photographic memory, do all your required reading with a pencil and sheet of notebook paper at your side. Use the notebook sheet as a bookmark. As you come to important parts of the book, write down the page numbers and phrases that describe the passages, quotations, and scenes you may want to use in your paper later on. If you do this conscientiously, you will have all the information you need to write a first-rate paper by the time you finish the book.

Listed here are guidelines for evaluating novels, biographies, plays, and books of nonfiction. Write down these guideline entries on your bookmark sheet and complete them as you read along. (You will find definitions for literary terms like plot, theme, narrator, etc., in Chapter 5.)

BOOKMARK SHEET
Guidelines for
Evaluating a Novel

Plot:
1. What are the most significant incidents in the book?

2. What is the main conflict of the book?
3. What is the climax of the story?
4. How does the novel end?
5. Is the plot predictable or unpredictable?

Characters:
1. List the names of all the main characters. Write down one significant trait about each one and the page number(s) of a passage or quotation that best reveals the kind of person that character is.
2. In what ways do the main characters change, if at all?
3. Does the author develop the characters well enough so that you can imagine them existing outside the novel? Give reasons for your answer.
4. Complete this sentence about one or two main characters:

_____ is the kind of person who
(name of character)

_____

Theme:
1. What is the author's theme, main idea, or message? (List the page numbers of quotations or passages in which the author states or implies the theme.)

Setting:
1. When and where does the story take place?
2. What are the most important settings?

Mood, Tone, and Style:
1. What is the overall mood of the book? (hu-

morous? optimistic? depressing? entertaining? preachy? informative?)

General Reaction:
1. This book made me realize that _____
   _____
   _____
2. The most memorable line in the book is: __
   _____
3. I ____would ____would not recommend this
   book to anyone who _____
   _____

BOOKMARK SHEET
Guidelines for
Evaluating
a Biography
or Autobiography

1. Write down the name, birthplace and birthday, and the names of parents, brothers, and sisters of the subject of the book.
2. List at least three or four major events in the subject's life. (Write down page numbers. You can find the relevant page numbers in the index of the book.)
3. List three or four major achievements and contributions the subject made. (List page numbers or check the index.)
4. List three or four setbacks and disappointments in the subject's life and the ways he or she dealt with them. (Write down page numbers or check the index.)

5. What were the subject's ideals? (List page numbers of statements the subject made or actions he or she performed that reveal these ideals.)

General Reaction:
1. Reading about _____ helped me
   (subject's name)
   see that _____
2. The subject's most memorable statement is:
   _____
   _____

BOOKMARK SHEET
Guidelines for
Evaluating a Play

1. Sum up the main conflict of the play. (List pages or lines where this is revealed.)
2. List the main characters. Next to each one write down a page number or line that reveals each character's personality.
3. Describe the most important scene in the play. (List page numbers.)
4. What is the author's main theme? (Write down page numbers or lines that reveal the theme.)

General Reaction:
1. The most important line in this play is: ___
   _____
2. If I were _____ in the
   (name of main character)
   play _____, I would have
   (name of play)
   _____

3. After reading _____,
(name of play)
   I _____would _____would not want to see it
   performed on stage because _____
   _____

BOOKMARK SHEET
Guidelines for
Evaluating
Nonfiction Books

1. What type of nonfiction book is this? (self-help? how-to? reference? history? political analysis?)
2. What got you interested in reading this particular book?
3. What do you think the author's main purpose was in writing this book? (List the page number where the author's purpose is stated; it is usually found in the preface or introduction.)
4. What use can you make of the information in this book?
5. List one important, startling, useful, or incredible thing you learned from this book.

General Reaction:
1. The kind of reader who would gain something from reading _____ is some-
(name of book)
   one who _____
   _____

2. This book helped me learn to see that _____
   _____
   _____

18

Take a break. Once you have filled out one of these bookmark forms, you are more than half-way toward completing your book report. You have done the reading, taken notes on all the important information in your book, focused on the main ideas, and sorted out your reactions. Turn to the next chapter to see how to use the information you have gathered for your paper.

Chapter 3

WRITING TIME: Organizing and Writing Essay-Style Reports, Plot Summaries, Critiques, and Oral Book Reports

ORGANIZING AND WRITING ESSAY-STYLE REPORTS

While many teachers occasionally assign book reports in the form of art projects, dramatic presentations, and other offbeat styles, the standard essay-style book report is still alive and well in English classrooms everywhere. In this kind of paper, you are asked to present a well-thought-out opinion (also called a thesis statement) about the book you read. Then you are expected to develop and support that opinion with examples from the book.

Sounds pretty straightforward, doesn't it? One main idea supported by several related ones. Yet this is just the kind of report that stumps many students. They wonder how they are going to get an entire book into a short, focused paper. It is a tricky assignment that takes some planning. Let's look at the steps involved in preparing this kind of report. So far we've covered the following steps:

Step 1: Write down all the information about the assignment.

Step 2: Make up a schedule for writing the report.

Step 3: Plan your reading.

Step 4: Begin reading, taking notes as you do so.

Once you have taken detailed notes on your bookmark sheet, you are ready for the next step.

Step 5: Develop a thesis statement.

What is a thesis statement anyway, and how do you come up with one? The thesis of your paper states your topic and purpose. It is the guiding idea for your entire report—a kind of "umbrella" statement under which everything else fits.

To come up with a good thesis, study your notes, then ask yourself this question: "What is the number-one thing I want to say about this book?" Did the book teach you something you didn't know before? Give you insights about human behavior? Show you characters who represent certain values? Introduce you to new experiences and places?

Here are a few guidelines for writing a useful thesis statement:

★ Write your statement in a declarative sentence, not in a question or a phrase.
★ Write a statement that covers *only* what you plan to develop and discuss in your report.
★ Write a statement that is somewhat open to argument so that the reader will be curious to see how you support that argument. For example, "Huck Finn is a true rebel." "*Animal Farm* is not really about animals."

Once you have a thesis statement, think about what parts of the book tie in with what you have stated. For example, if your main impression of a novel is that it taught you about human greed, what parts of the book led you to that conclusion? The characters? The narrator's comments? Once again, study your notes, looking for examples from the book that support your thesis. This brings us to Step 6.

Step 6: Use your notes to make up an outline.

With your thesis statement before you, go

through your notes again and put a check next to any items that tie in with your thesis. At this stage, you probably have a few additional thoughts about the book. Write them down on your bookmark sheet before you forget them—just a phrase will do. At this stage you are gathering as much related information as possible with which to support your thesis.

Once you have checked off usable information, ideas, passages, quotations, and details from your notes, you are ready to make up an outline.

An outline is really a road map showing where you plan to go. While some writers work out the order of their ideas in several rough drafts, you will save yourself a lot of time if you get your ideas in order ahead of time. It's a lot easier to juggle ideas and supporting information in a one-page outline than to do cut-and-paste revisions in a rough draft of several pages.

If you find the standard outline form a little too formal, then simply list all your ideas and supporting information in the order you plan to follow on your paper.

If you would like to organize your ideas in a regular outline, see page 64.

To fill in your outline, group ideas from your notes into categories. Eliminate those that don't really fit into your groupings.

Once you have decided on your categories, it's time to think about how you want to arrange them. Here are several ways to consider organizing your outline and report:

★ Chronological order
★ Order of importance

★ Comparison and contrast
★ General to specific
★ Cause and effect

If you have completed all the steps so far, you only need two or three more nights to finish your paper—one night to write a rough draft and another to rewrite and polish your report.

Step 7: Write a rough draft.

THE OPENING PARAGRAPH:

The most important section of your book report is the introductory paragraph. It is also the hardest to write because it has to do so many jobs: establish the main idea of your paper, set the tone, and make the reader want to read more.

If you want to keep your reader awake, here are some openers to *avoid:*

"In this report, I'm going to discuss . . ."
"This report is about . . ."
"I think . . ."

Don't say what you are going to do, just do it right from the beginning, and your paper will begin on a real note of authority.

Think of your opening sentence or paragraph as a headline that has to grab the reader's attention right away. Here are various types of openers to consider. The *Gone with the Wind* examples shown are based on the thesis statement: "Scarlett O'Hara, a legendary Southern belle, is one of the most liberated women in fiction." Keep in mind that your thesis statement is a *guiding idea* and not necessarily an actual sentence in your introduction.

★ *The startling statement:* "If Betty Friedan, Gloria Steinem, and Scarlett O'Hara were invited to the same party, they would have plenty in common to talk about."

★ *The question:* "Who would imagine finding such a contemporary woman as Scarlett O'Hara in a novel as traditional and old-fashioned as *Gone with the Wind?*"

★ *The story opener:* "Long before there was a region we call the New South, there was an Old South characterized by genteel women, and in that mannered society a feisty and independent Scarlett O'Hara was reared."

Once you have an attention-getting opener, work on the rest of your introduction. Make sure your paragraph includes the name of the book and its author, your main idea, and a hint of how you plan to develop your idea with supporting information from the book. Here is an example of an introductory paragraph about *Gone with the Wind* that includes all these points:

> Who would imagine finding such a contemporary woman as Scarlett O'Hara in a novel as traditional and old-fashioned as *Gone with the Wind*? In the character of Scarlett, Margaret Mitchell has created a heroine whose determination, shrewdness, and common sense make it possible for her to survive the loss of her home and the deaths of her parents, two husbands, and a child, and still say: "Tomorrow is another day."

THE MIDDLE:

An effective opening paragraph sets up your entire paper. With it, you capture your reader's attention. Your next job is to maintain the reader's interest over the course of five or six paragraphs in which you develop each of the ideas on your outline.

The middle section is where you weave in all the quotations, anecdotes, details, and reasons you listed in your notes and outline. This is where you convince the reader of the truth of your opening sentence.

The body of your paper should convey a real feeling about the book with key quotations and passages that bring the book to life. Make the characters *talk.* Help the reader *picture* the setting you read about. Make your reader *think* about the author's important ideas.

THE ENDING:

Once you have developed each point in your outline, it's time to end your report. Avoid trailing off, stopping abruptly, or rehashing your thesis statement again. Your conclusion should leave your reader with a satisfied feeling that you have tied together all your earlier ideas.

This can be tricky. One way to do it is to end with an appropriate quotation from the book. You can also end your paper by echoing your thesis statement in a clincher sentence. Example: "And so, in the unlikeliest of places and times, we've met a woman who was not only on an equal footing with the men of her time but would be so with the men of today."

Once you have written your conclusion, take a one-night break before moving on to the next step. After a breather, you will have a better idea of what works and what needs cutting or polishing.

Step 8: Revise and proofread your rough draft.

If you have followed all the suggested steps so far, your rough draft is probably in fairly good shape. So why not turn it in as is? You could, and you would probably get a pretty decent grade. But the point of this book is to help you turn in the best possible paper. And that means rewriting and polishing your rough draft.

Now is the time to smooth out any wrinkles you couldn't get to the first time around. This is the stage where you check that you have moved smoothly from one idea to the next so that the reader can do the same. If you always spell *deceive* wrong, and it's in your paper, this is your chance to catch the error before your teacher does.

Now are you convinced? If so, use the following checklist as a guide for editing the content, style, and organization of your report. Use the proofreader's sheet in Chapter 5 to make your job easier. Get yourself a red pencil for marking your paper, a pair of scissors and tape in case you want to rearrange paragraphs, a good dictionary to check on spelling, and a thesaurus to change a good word to a better one. Here goes:

EDITING FOR CONTENT:

	Yes	Needs fixing
1. My topic and purpose are very clear.	____	____
2. I have written an attention-getting first paragraph.	____	____
3. I have supported my main idea with specific material from the book.	____	____
4. All the quoted material is accurate.	____	____
5. There is a clear focal point to my paper.	____	____
6. All the information I have included is relevant to the main topic.	____	____

EDITING FOR ORGANIZATION:

	Yes	Needs fixing
1. Each paragraph presents one idea related to the central topic.	____	____
2. My ideas are arranged and developed logically.	____	____
3. I have used connecting words to help the reader move smoothly from one paragraph to the next.	____	____
4. My conclusion brings the report to a clear, satisfying end.	____	____

EDITING FOR STYLE:

	Yes	Needs fixing
1. I have said *exactly* what I mean throughout the report.	――	――
2. The tone I have used is appropriate to my topic and to the book I have written about.	――	――
3. I have used specific, concrete words.	――	――
4. I have used strong, active verbs.	――	――
5. I have worked quotations and passages smoothly into my paper.	――	――
6. I have varied my choice of words, phrases, and sentences.	――	――
7. I have avoided jargon and clichés.	――	――

EDITING FOR GRAMMAR AND MECHANICS:

1. I have indented all paragraphs.	――	――
2. All my sentences are capitalized.	――	――
3. All my sentences end with appropriate punctuation.	――	――
4. I have checked the spelling of tricky words.	――	――

5. All the quotations I used are in quotation marks. _____ _____
6. All verbs agree with their subjects, and verb tenses and pronoun agreements are consistent. _____ _____

Step 9: Write the final draft.

You are all set. Simply make the changes you indicated on your rough draft when you recopy your paper. Do a quick run-through to make sure you have changed everything you intended to fix. Add a cover and page numbers if your teacher requested them. You're done. Good luck!

Step 10: Turn your paper in on time. (And relax!)

ORGANIZING AND WRITING A PLOT SUMMARY

If you are reading this section count your blessings, because you have a much easier job than the student who has to write an essay-style book report. Your teacher has already made the biggest decision for you—that you will write about the plot and only the plot.

You don't have to make judgments about the characters, you simply have to describe them. You aren't required to figure out the theme but just have to present events in the order in which they took place. A few lines about the setting completes your plot summary.

You will find a section about note-taking earlier, in Chapter 2. Again use a notebook sheet as a bookmark and complete these questions on your sheet.

BOOKMARK SHEET
Guidelines for
Writing a
Plot Summary

1. List the names of all the main characters and a descriptive phrase about each one.
2. Describe the opening scene in one sentence.
3. Describe the conflict of the book in one sentence.
4. Describe the climax or high point of the book in one sentence.
5. Describe the conclusion of the book.
6. For each chapter, make up a time line that looks like this:

    Chapter 1—opening scene
    characters presented
    one or two incidents
    one useful quotation (page number)

Once you have finished reading the book and have completed your bookmark sheet, start writing your summary. Write one paragraph for each chapter, but don't refer to the chapter specifically or you will bore your reader.

What you are working for is a miniature version of the book—the highlights presented in the same sequence as the original. Think of your plot summary as a book jacket or catalogue card. You want the basics, plus a flavor of the book, which you can achieve with one or two apt quotations and a couple of concise descriptions of the characters.

Try to weave in, as naturally as possible, your quotations and character descriptions. "Rhett Butler, a handsome rogue and a daring Confederate gunrunner . . ." offers just the right amount of information for a plot summary.

Conclude your summary by describing the windup of the book, and you're done!

ORGANIZING AND WRITING A CRITIQUE

In a critique, you are expected to present your opinions, criticisms, and recommendations based on specific examples from the book. Here is how to organize and write one.

BOOKMARK SHEET
Guidelines for
Writing a Critique

1. On your bookmark sheet, list all your opin-

ions about the book. Next to each opinion, write down the page reference of a specific quotation, incident, or description that influenced your opinion. Include opinions about the book's plot, characters, themes, setting, and style.

2. Rearrange your opinions in the most effective order possible. You can do this in list or outline form.

3. With your ordered list or outline before you, write your lead sentence. Make sure you state clearly where you stand on the subject.

4. Show, don't tell. Write supporting sentences and paragraphs that show exactly why you hold these opinions.

5. Write a concluding sentence that summarizes all your opinions and lets the reader know exactly how you feel about the book. Based on your critique, the reader should feel moved either to run out and get the book or to avoid it completely.

6. Proofread your rough draft and rewrite it.

ORGANIZING AND PRESENTING AN ORAL BOOK REPORT

Coming down with a mysterious illness is one way to avoid an oral book report. So is a blizzard or hurricane. But you don't have to pray for a disaster to cope with this kind of report. Here's some advice.

Find a book you really feel strongly about. Decide in no uncertain terms why you love (or hate) the book. Decide that you want your audience to love or hate it, too.

To get started, use one of these surefire openers:

★ Ask a provocative question of your audience: "How would you like to stay up all night reading one of the scariest books ever written?"

★ Read an exciting, moving, or special passage from the book.

★ Prepare a brief plot summary leading up to the climax of the book, read it, then ask your audience to guess the outcome of the book.

Whatever opener you use, decide beforehand how you will begin. Write your main points and quotations on note cards. Then tape your report or present it to a family member or friend a few times so that you can begin to "hear" it in your mind.

Right before you give your talk, take a few deep breaths to slow yourself down. As you speak, don't be afraid to pause once in a while. Give your audience a chance to take in what you've said. Avoid the temptation to fill up the blank spots with *uh*s and *uhm*s.

If you are using note cards, look up from them frequently to keep up eye contact with your audience. Use hand gestures to emphasize your main points.

Plan a definite conclusion that sums up your opinions. Don't trail off, or your audience will, too. End with a smile and exit with confidence.

If all these measures fail, ask your teacher if you can tape your book talk instead and donate the tape to your classroom or school library.

Chapter 4

ON THE BOOKS: All Kinds of Book Report Topics

Do you panic if your teacher announces, "For this assignment, you can choose your own kind of book report to turn in"? You know someone in the class will do some fabulous art project that will go on display. And a couple of drama-group students will probably put on a Broadway-caliber performance of a scene from a book. You want to do something original, too, but you may be stumped for ideas.

Here's help. This chapter is filled with dozens of book report ideas that will get you out of the rut for good. If you are a literary type, there are all sorts of writing ideas for novels and plays. For artistic students and those with dramatic leanings, there are a number of original projects to work on. And if you think that two or more heads are better than one, there is even a selection of group book report projects to work on.

Whatever you choose, do check in with your teacher about your plans. A senior honors English teacher might not be too impressed with a papier mâché set of the characters in *Little Women*. By the same token, a seventh-grader might find it rough going if he or she set out to write a paper on the literary symbolism in *Lord of the Flies*. So look for topics that are fun, interesting, *and* appropriate.

NOVEL BOOK REPORTS

Sometimes your teacher will ask you for a book report that gives a general overview of all the aspects of the assigned novel: the plot; the characters; the theme; the setting; its tone, mood, and style; and its point of view. Sometimes you may be expected to cover only one of these topics but in greater depth. Here are some ideas for all of these assignments.

The Whole Book

ESSAY-STYLE WRITING TOPICS:
★ In a well-written novel, all the various elements of the book fit together and have a reason for existing. Pick several events, characters, or passages and discuss why they are necessary to the novel you have read. If, on the other hand, you feel there are parts of the book that don't fit or don't really work, describe what they are and why they detract from the work.

★ An author makes himself or herself known through the characters, events, and narrative descriptions in the novel. From these three areas, decide what you think are the author's *personal* moral views and standards. Use quotations from the book to support your opinions.

★ The narrator is the key figure in most novels. Some narrators speak as third-person outsiders (omniscient observers), who see all the actions of all the characters, but are not actual characters in the story themselves. Other narrators are actually main or secondary characters in the novel who speak in the first person "I." In the book you have read, what role does the narrator play? Is he or she an insider or an outside observer? If the narrator switched from third person to first or vice versa, how would that change the tone of the novel?

★ Even in a fantasy, the world the author presents in the novel must be consistent and believable and make the reader feel that he or she is part of that world. In your report, discuss whether you were able to become part of a believable world in the book you read or whether the world of the novel was inconsistent, unbelievable, or incomplete in parts. Be sure to support your views with evidence from the book.

★ Quote the most significant passage or line in the book and explain its importance.

★ Do you think you will remember this book a year from now? If you think so, cite which parts of the book make it memorable. If you think the book will be forgotten in a year, discuss the book's weaknesses. If the book isn't really memorable, but provides good temporary entertainment, say exactly why you think so.

★ Discuss whether the book you read appeals to your intellect, your feelings, your imagination, or a combination of all three.

ACTIVITIES:

★ Imagine that the book you read was just published this year. As a prominent book critic, you have been asked to send in a one- or two-page recommendation of a book to be considered for the Pulitzer Prize in fiction. What would you say about the book? (If this book is not a worthy candidate, write a rejection of it instead.)

★ Imagine that the author of the book you have read is coming to your class. Make up a list of ten thought-provoking questions you would like him or her to answer for you and other readers.

★ You are an editor at a publishing company. Imagine that the book you have read arrives in manuscript form on your desk. Write a letter to the author saying why you will or will not publish the manuscript. Include suggestions of how the book might be improved.

★ Make up a report card evaluating various elements of the book you have read. Give a letter grade for each of the following: plot, characters, theme, style, setting. Write one paragraph explaining why you gave each grade.

★ Develop a study and activity sheet for other readers interested in reading the same book. Include at least ten essay questions, twenty multiple choice questions about the characters, plot, and setting, and two or three writing activities.

★ Write a paper stating why your book would be enjoyed by one who usually hates reading.

Plot

ESSAY-STYLE WRITING TOPICS:

★ What is the opening scene of the plot? Tell why it did or did not interest you in reading further.

★ What is the main turning point in the plot? Discuss how characters and situations changed after this turning point.

★ Is the plot predictable or unpredictable? Give reasons for your answer.

★ Describe the ending of the book, then discuss whether it ended in a satisfying way or not. Mention other ways the author might have ended the story instead.

★ Discuss two or three of the most interesting and memorable incidents in the book. Give reasons for your choices.

★ Does the book end because the characters determine the ending, or does the author depend on plot development and resolution to end the book?

★ Is the plot believable, suspenseful, and interesting enough to keep you turning the pages? Give reasons for your answers based on events in the book.

★ Is the plot unified so that the book has a clear beginning, middle, and end? Do the subplots tie in smoothly? Support your answer with evidence from the book.

ACTIVITIES:

★ Draw up a sequential list of all the main events that comprise the plot. Next to each entry, write a paragraph stating the significance of each event to the story.

★ Describe how changing or removing one important incident would have altered the subsequent events in the book.

★ Write an epilogue to the book that takes place five years after the events in the actual conclusion.

★ Write a new ending to the book.

★ Write a scenario describing the plot for a producer of a television mini-series. You may follow the original sequence of the book or alter the order of events through possible flashbacks. You may also add new scenes or drop existing ones to make your scenario more appealing.

★ Develop a scene that is mentioned but not really shown in the book. Before you actually write the scene, tell your reader what the scene is and write down the paragraph in which it is mentioned.

★ Think up a new adventure or incident to add to the book. Write it up as a passage or a separate chapter.

★ Design a bookmark for the book which includes a plot summary of 100 words or less.

Characters

ESSAY-STYLE WRITING TOPICS:

★ Discuss the author's attitude toward one of the main characters. (Is the author friendly, exasperated, scornful, envious, sympathetic, loving, unkind, disapproving, or admiring toward this character?) In what specific ways do you discover the author's attitude? Use examples of description, dialogue, or narration to support your opinion.

★ Think about the most interesting main character in the book. Does that character change or grow? What causes the change? Is it a positive or negative change?

★ What is the function of the minor characters? (To contrast with the main characters? Provide comic relief? Advance the plot? Give readers insights about a main character?)

★ Why do you think the main characters behave as they do? Give examples from the book to support your views.

★ What are the main characters' moral standards? What would they be likely to do in certain real-life situations you have been in?

★ What is the main character's most significant speech, line, or action in the book? Explain its importance.

★ Discuss whether the main characters, or the minor characters, are believable. Have you ever met people like them in your own life? Discuss similarities between these fictional characters and people you know.

★ Choose one main character to write about. How do you learn about this character? Through his or her actions and dialogue or through the author's descriptions of that character?

★ Think about a character from the book and the most significant thing he or she does. Then discuss what you think the character's motivation was for behaving that way.

★ Discuss the steps that led up to a character's making a particular choice.

★ Discuss an incident seen differently by two different characters.

★ Complete one of the following lines about

a character (or characters), and use this sentence as the first line of an essay about those characters:

1. Faced with the same conflict as

   _____,
   (name of character)
   I would have behaved differently.

2. If I had a chance to meet

   _____
   (name of character)
   face to face, I would want to know why

   _____

   _____

3. The main character of

   _____
   (name of novel)
   is the kind of person who _____

   _____

   _____

ACTIVITIES:

★ Imagine what one of the main characters of the book you have read would do offstage if:

1. he or she were given one wish.
2. he or she had a chance to "talk back" to the author.
3. he or she could make a different decision at a critical turning point.

★ Make a list of ten rules that the main character in the book lives by. Compare this with the rules other people in the book expect him or her to follow.

★ Write down four or five actions the main character would find impossible to do. Give reasons for your opinions.

★ If you had a chance to meet a character from

the book you read, what questions would you ask to determine why he or she behaved in a certain way?

★ Create a new character for the book you read. Discuss how that character would relate to the others and how he or she would affect the outcome of the story. Explain how, why, and where you would introduce your new character into the story line. Or recreate an actual scene from the book and put the new character in it with the existing characters.

★ In the role of one of the main characters undergoing a conflict in the book, write a "Dear Abby" letter explaining the problem. Then write an appropriate response suggesting ways the character might deal with it.

★ Take one or two main characters from the book you have read (or characters from different books) and put them into your own short story. Make sure they behave "in character" within the story.

★ As a director casting parts for a movie or television version of the book, tell which actors you would choose for the lead and supporting roles. Give reasons for your choices.

★ From the point of view of one of the characters, write a diary entry covering an important scene.

★ Write a newspaper obituary about one of the characters.

★ Locate a book of astrology that describes the supposed character traits of each birth sign. Then choose one sign that best fits each of the main characters. Give reasons for your choice.

★ You are an incorrigible matchmaker. Choose

two characters from two different books and explain why you think they would make a great match or become good friends.

Theme

ESSAY-STYLE WRITING TOPICS:

★ Discuss what insights you have gained about life by reading this book.

★ Choose one quotation or passage from the book that reflects what you consider to be the main theme or idea. Then discuss the significance of the passage.

★ What do you think is the author's most important message in the book? Do you agree or disagree with this theme? Give reasons for your answer.

★ Discuss whether or not the theme of the book is relevant to present-day life.

★ Complete one of the following lines and use it as the opening sentence of an essay-style report about the theme of the book you have read:

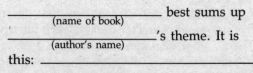

1. The ideals _____ writes
      (author's name)
   about in _____ have
      (name of book)
   led me to think about my own values.
2. One sentence (or paragraph) from

   _____ best sums up
      (name of book)
   _____'s theme. It is
      (author's name)
   this: _____

   _____

3. I could not ____agree ____disagree more
with the philosophy expressed by

_____ in
(author or main character)

_____ .
(name of book)

Setting

ESSAY-STYLE WRITING TOPICS:

★ Is the setting important to the story? Give
reasons for your answer.

★ Describe the most memorable settings of the
book and their significance to the story.

★ Is the setting a part of the mood of the story?
If so, analyze how the author uses setting to create
a particular feeling in the book.

ACTIVITIES:

★ If you are interested in design and have an
artistic eye and flair, recreate two or three of the
main settings of the book as a set designer would
render them for a play.

★ Imagine that you are a decorator and have
been asked to design and furnish a house for one
of the main characters. Describe the kind of setting you would create.

★ If one of the settings in the book you have
read is particularly exotic or interesting, write up
a travel brochure describing its appeal for a certain
kind of traveler.

★ Create a new cover for the book that gives a
reader a sense of the time and place of the book.

Tone, Mood, and Style

ESSAY-STYLE WRITING TOPICS:

★ Describe or write down the opening scene of the book. Then discuss how the opening sets the tone and mood of the rest of the book.

★ Does the author of the novel seem sympathetic to the characters? Use specific examples of the language the author uses to convey his attitude toward the characters.

★ How would you describe the mood of the book you have read? (mysterious? humorous? rollicking? gloomy? chaotic? mournful?) In a short essay, describe the overall mood and feeling of the book, giving examples that contribute to this mood.

ACTIVITIES:

★ If you were to turn an important scene in the book into a radio play, what music and sound effects would you use to convey the mood of the original book? Describe your plans for the play.

★ Picture yourself as the director of a movie based on the book you have read. You are meeting with the actors to help them act out the scene. What kinds of instructions would you give them to have them convey the appropriate tone of the original? How would you have them move or talk?

★ If you have a special interest in music, plan what music you would choose as the score of a movie based on the book.

Point of View

ESSAY-STYLE WRITING TOPICS:

★ From whose point of view is the story told?

If the story were told from a different point of view, how would that have changed the novel?

★ Discuss how two separate characters react differently to the same event in the book. Mention the reasons for each one's interpretation of that event.

ACTIVITIES:

★ Take an important scene from the book and rewrite it from another point of view. If, for example, it is written from the first-person perspective of one of the characters, have another character tell the story. Or change from the first-person viewpoint to the third-person or vice versa.

★ Choose two characters from the book and have them write character sketches of each other.

BIOGRAPHY AND AUTOBIOGRAPHY BOOK REPORTS

ESSAY-STYLE WRITING TOPICS:

★ Why is the subject of the biography or autobiography worthy of being written or read about?

★ What are the subject's most notable achievements?

★ What were the subject's early goals and ideals? Did he or she succeed in reaching them?

★ Discuss the specific influences of the subject's family, education, friends, society, social position, and religion on his or her life.

★ Explain what contributions the subject of the biography or autobiography made to society, politics, art, sports, or his or her area of expertise.

★ What is the subject's most memorable quotation or speech? Show how the subject's actions or ideals are exemplified in that quotation.

★ In an anecdote, describe an incident that shows an *unexpected* side to the subject's personality.

★ In an anecdote, describe an incident that shows a *typical* trait of the subject.

★ What setbacks did the subject experience that formed his or her character? How did the subject deal with these setbacks?

★ What were the major turning points in the subject's life? How did the subject behave at these times?

★ What was the subject's greatest strength? Greatest weakness? Compare these two sides of the subject's character.

★ What was the subject's single greatest achievement? Failure? Compare these two events.

★ From reading the introduction or preface to the biography, why do you think the author chose to write about the subject? What were the author's special qualifications and sources? Do you think the author was objective and fair in writing about the subject?

★ Elaborate on one of the following lines and use it as the opening sentence for your report:

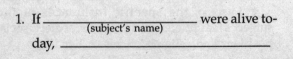

1. If _____ were alive to-
   (subject's name)
   day, _____

2. Even a great life is filled with ordinary events.
3. Sometimes a twist of fate turns an unremarkable life into an extraordinary one.

ACTIVITIES:

★ Choose one main incident from the biography you read. Then read other accounts of that event in other biographies, or in magazine and newspaper articles from that period. Then write a report in which you discuss how accurately the author of the book you read described the incident.

★ Prepare a time line of the major events in the subject's life, writing a short paragraph next to the major entries.

★ Write a *Who's Who?* account of the subject of the biography or autobiography you read. Go to your local or school library to read up on the style and content of a typical *Who's Who?* entry.

★ Write an obituary of the person you read about based on the information in the biography.

★ Make up a set of tough questions you might ask the subject if he or she were to be interviewed on *Meet the Press, Face the Nation*, or *60 Minutes*.

BOOK REPORTS ABOUT PLAYS

ESSAY-STYLE WRITING TOPICS:

★ What is the main conflict of the play? How is the conflict resolved?

★ What is the main theme or message of the play? Does a character state the theme, or does the reader have to figure out what the theme is from many different elements in the play?

★ Describe the most important scene in the play and the reasons for its significance.

★ Quote the most memorable line or lines in the play and discuss why they are important.

★ In a play, you only learn about the characters from their lines and from what other characters say about them. Write a short character sketch for two of the main characters based on what you learn from them in the play *and* what you imagine them to be like outside the play.

★ Find lines in the play that explain why a main character behaves in a particular way and discuss them.

★ Discuss whether you would like to see a live production of this play.

ACTIVITIES:

★ If the ending of the play you read is in any way unsatisfactory, change the last scene or add a new one to change the outcome of the play.

★ Rewrite the play as a short story.

★ Write a new character into one of the play's scenes.

★ Plan a production of the play (or just a scene from it) for your class. Decide on casting, sets, costumes, direction, etc. Write up your plans on a production sheet. Better yet, put on the play or scene!

★ Make a shadow box of the most important scene or scenes in each act.

★ Do a reading of an important scene in the play, tape it, then discuss the significance of that scene.

★ As a Hollywood producer, you are interested in making a film of the play in question. Because of the greater resources you have, you can shoot scenes on location, have more flexibility with characters, compress scenes, use flashbacks more liberally, etc. Write up a description of how you would produce the play as a movie. Keep in mind that the language of a play intended only for the stage often sounds "stilted" or "stagey" in another medium. Discuss some of the lines you plan to adapt or take out, as well as other alterations you will have to make to the play.

NONFICTION BOOK REPORTS

ESSAY-STYLE WRITING TOPICS:

★ What was the author's purpose in writing this book and your reasons for reading it? Did the author succeed in his effort and you in yours?

★ Name five important facts you discovered in the book and the reasons you think they are important.

★ If the book is a "how-to" or "self-help" book, do you think the advice was worthwhile? Give reasons for your answers.

★ What are the main points that the author makes in the book?

★ Discuss who you think the ideal reader is for this book.

★ Complete these statements and use one of them as an introductory sentence in a report:

1. The kind of reader who would appreciate
_____ is someone who
   (name of book)
_____
_____.

2. One startling fact I learned from reading
_____
   (name of book)
is _____
_____.

SCIENCE FICTION BOOK REPORTS

ESSAY-STYLE WRITING TOPICS:

★ Describe the time and place of the book you have read.

★ Discuss the theme of the science fiction book you have read.

★ Discuss the most suspenseful and surprising parts of the story.

★ Explain why you would or would not want to live during the time or in one of the places described in the book.

ACTIVITIES:

★ Imagine you are a scout or a reporter sent to the world depicted in the book. Write a report based on your findings. Include information about the world's inhabitants, atmosphere, social and political structure, etc.

★ Illustrate some of the strange creatures from the book based on the author's descriptions of them.

★ Create a sci-fi comic strip based on events and characters in the book.

★ Make up a list of questions you would ask one of the aliens if he or she or it dropped in for a visit, assuming, of course, that you would be able to understand one another.

★ Plan the production of a super space-epic movie along the lines of *Star Wars*. In a report discuss which scenes you will include, whom you will cast in the movie, the kind of music you will use, and the kinds of settings and costumes you will design.

MYSTERY BOOK REPORT TOPICS

★ Invent a crime to be solved by the same detective as the one in the mystery you read. Then write a short story in which that detective has to crack the case.

★ Write a newspaper article about the crime that occurred in the mystery you read and a follow-up showing how it was solved.

★ You have decided that what television needs is one more cop show. To make your presentation to the networks, write a "treatment" describing how this book will be the basis for an episode of your show. What scenes will you include? Whom will you cast as the characters? What other kinds of crimes will the sleuth have to solve in later episodes?

ROMANCE BOOK REPORT TOPICS

★ Create a computer dating questionnaire and fill it out for each of the main characters in the book. Include questions about each character's appearance, interests, hobbies, pet peeves, and passions, along with questions that explore what the character is looking for in a mate.

★ In an original short story that you write, introduce one of the characters in your romance to a character of the opposite sex whom you create.

★ Compile an anthology of poems, songs, and pictures that deal with the romantic themes in the book you have read.

SUPERNATURAL, HORROR, AND OCCULT BOOK REPORT TOPICS

★ Create a radio script including sound effects and music that are appropriate to a particularly spooky scene in a book you have read.

★ Imagine you are a scientist or doctor who has been called in to explain the unusual events in the book. Write a scientific or medical report expressing your views.

★ Write a newspaper account of the unusual events in the book you have read.

ALL KINDS OF
ART PROJECT
BOOK REPORTS

★ Design a store-window display to sell the book. Create a new book cover, illustrate a poster, recreate some scenes in shadow boxes or on poster board, use objects as symbols of various elements of the book. You may even want to work on this project with your teacher or librarian so that you can actually create a display right in your school.

★ If the book you have read has a particularly exotic theme or takes place in an interesting time or place, plan a theme party or dance. Make up a list of fictional characters who should be invited, design the decor, plan the music, and think of an appropriate menu.

★ Create a complete bulletin-board display of your book for your classroom, library, or hallway. Include inspirational quotations from the book, intriguing passages that will make other students want to read the book, illustrations, etc.

★ If your book is an adventure, make up a map that shows the locale of various important scenes in the book. Use small illustrations on the map to indicate various events in the book.

★ Illustrate a poster based on one important quotation from the book.

★ Make up a collage that represents various elements in the book: characters, settings, quotations, symbols, etc.

★ Make up a special bookmark for the book that will intrigue the next reader.

★ Find or take photographs that evoke the feeling of certain scenes or passages in the book you have read. Collect these pictures in a folder and write down the scene or passage each photo illustrates.

★ If the book you have read is especially adventurous, make up a comic book or comic strip that depicts an exciting scene.

★ Draw a family tree showing the relationships among related characters in the story.

★ Make up a scrapbook about the book you have read. Include quotations, pictures, photos, and memorabilia that give a feeling of the book.

★ Create a wall mural that depicts the action of an exciting section of the book.

ALL KINDS OF DRAMATIC BOOK REPORTS

★ Pick a favorite scene from the book you have read and write a short script based on it. Then, with the help of another student, act out the script in front of your class, or tape it for the class.

★ Do a reading of a particularly atmospheric or suspenseful part of the book. Make a tape of sound effects or appropriate music to accompany the reading.

★ Many books have been adapted into musicals. Do you think the book you read would lend itself to musical treatment? If so, write the lyrics for three or four songs to be used in several key scenes in a musical based on the book.

★ Trace the life of a fictional character or the subject of a biography in a *This Is Your Life* television program. You may need to enlist the help of other students to act as key figures from the person's life.

★ Find a student who had an opposite reaction from yours to the book you read. Then debate this statement: "This book is so good that it should not be required reading for our class."

★ Write a monologue of the personal thoughts of one of the characters in a key scene from the book. Then read or tape your monologue for the class. Be sure to describe the events that lead up to the monologue.

ALL KINDS OF GROUP-PROJECT BOOK REPORTS

★ With other students in the class, make up questions to fire at the author of or a character in a book that several of you have read. Appoint one person to play the role of the author or character while the rest of you enact the roles of reporters. Then conduct a *Meet the Press* program for the rest of the class.

★ Plan a party for fictional characters from various books you and several other students have read. Assign the following tasks to members of your group: Write a short paper explaining why these characters were invited; write an individual letter to each person on the list inviting him or her to the party; write a one-act play about the actual party; write a gossip column describing this unusual social gathering.

★ With other members of your class, write an entire front page for a newspaper based on the major events in a book all of you have read or on important incidents in different books. Agree on the format, design, layout, and content of all the articles.

★ Each person in the class writes a short report on an index card to be used for reference when students are looking for good books to read. Each card should include the following information:

Title, author, reviewer's name in corner

Brief plot summary in five to six sentences

Description of four main characters

Rating: A. Terrific
        B. O.K.
        C. Don't bother

☐ I recommend this book because
_____

_____

☐ I do not recommend this book because _____

_____

The cards will be kept on file in the classroom or school library.

★ Groups of students who have read the same book plan a comprehensive bulletin-board display to interest other readers in reading the book. Include teaser questions, plot summaries, illustrations of key scenes, important quotations, materials that symbolize various objects in the book, photos, etc. Your group might even want to consider creating a tape of some aspect of the book.

★ With other students in your class, organize a "Class Book Award" ceremony. Each student nominates a favorite book for an award, giving reasons for his or her choice. The teacher decides which book wins the award based on the effectiveness of the presentations. To throw some humor into the presentations, you might want to award booby prizes as well (corniest situation, most unbelievable character, most predictable plot, book most likely to cure insomnia, etc.).

★ Students who have all read the same book construct a board game based on the book. Use Monopoly as a model for the board and game cards.

★ Students who have all read the same book become experts on one part of the book: setting, theme, plot, characters, etc., and then prepare an oral presentation or a written report on the aspect of the book they chose. A variation on this is to have the group prepare a "book preview" package to spark another reader's interest in the book. The package would contain a bookmark with a plot summary, a new book jacket complete with blurbs, a copy of a key passage or scene, a list of the main characters, and a list of provocative questions that might interest a curious reader. An elaborate package might also include a taped reading of an exciting scene and one or two objects or clues which the reader will have to find in the book.

ORAL BOOK REPORT TOPICS

★ Make up a tape for your school or classroom library describing the plot, characters, setting, and highlights of the book you have read. Read at least one key passage and tell the listener why you recommend the book.

★ Write, then read to the class a short, exciting synopsis of the book leading up to an important scene or passage which you also read aloud. Then ask the class to speculate on the outcome of the plot. This activity can be performed live or on tape.

★ Write a two-minute radio or television commercial "selling" the book to the audience. Use props, visual aids, and taped sound effects to make your commercial convincing.

★ Read your favorite passage from the book aloud and explain why you chose it.

★ Write up a list of provocative questions to be directed to the author or a character in the book. Then have a friend or your teacher ask the questions which you will answer in the author or character's role.

★ You are a salesperson working for the publisher of the book you have read. Prepare a sales pitch to be delivered before a group of booksellers, convincing them to stock this book in their stores. Use visual aids to strengthen your talk.

OTHER BOOK REPORT PROJECTS

★ Research the life of the author of the book you have read and write a mini-biography of that person.

★ Make up a list of twenty questions and/or riddles that a reader should be able to answer upon completing the book. Be sure to include three or four essay-style discussion questions as well.

★ Write a diary, journal, or newspaper account covering a critical period in the book you have read.

★ Create a puzzle which a reader should be able to complete after reading the book.

★ If you have seen a film version of the book you have read, write a report comparing the book and movie.

★ Write a letter to a friend recommending the book or discouraging your friend from reading it.

★ If your book is written in an eccentric or unusual style, write a parody of an important scene in the book.

★ Find twenty-five difficult vocabulary words in the book, look them up, and write definitions for them.

★ Rewrite the ending of the book.

★ Write an original poem, play, or story inspired by the book you have read.

Chapter 5

BOOKENDS: A Complete Book Report Survival Kit

10 STEPS TO WRITING A BOOK REPORT

A Checklist

Step 1: Write down all the information about the assignment. _____

Step 2: Make up a schedule for writing the report. _____

Step 3: Plan your reading. _____

Step 4: Begin reading, taking notes as you do so. _____

Step 5: Develop a thesis statement. _____

Step 6: Use your notes to make up an outline. _____

Step 7: Write a rough draft. _____

Step 8: Revise and proofread your rough draft. _____

Step 9: Write the final draft. _____

Step 10: Turn your paper in on time. _____

BOOK REPORT SCHEDULE

A Checklist

Jobs to be done:	Due date:	Completed:
1. Get the assignment and know what is required.	_____	_____
2. Find at least two possible books and check them out with teacher.	_____	_____
3. Start reading. Schedule time by dividing number of pages by number of days before due date, allowing 4 to 5 days for writing.	_____	_____
4. Finish reading and take detailed notes on book.	_____	_____
5. Decide on topic and check it out with teacher.	_____	_____
6. Make up outline.	_____	_____
7. Write rough draft.	_____	_____
8. Proofread rough draft.	_____	_____
9. Rewrite rough draft.	_____	_____
10. Complete paper and turn it in.	_____	_____

OUTLINE FORM

The form below is a model for organizing a standard written book report. You may want to add other categories or adapt the form to suit your topic.

Thesis statement: _____

_____

I. _____
  A. _____
    1. _____
    2. _____
  B. _____
    1. _____
    2. _____
  C. _____
    1. _____
    2. _____

II. _____
  A. _____
    1. _____
    2. _____
  B. _____
    1. _____
    2. _____
  C. _____
    1. _____
    2. _____

III. _____
  A. _____
    1. _____
    2. _____

B. _____
  1. _____
  2. _____
C. _____
  1. _____
  2. _____

A SUGGESTED READING LIST

The following is a list of suggested books for your reference.

Alive by Piers Paul Read.
All Creatures Great and Small /All Things Bright and Beautiful by James Herriot.
All Quiet on the Western Front by Eric Remarque.
The Amityville Horror by Jay Anson.
Animal Farm by George Orwell.
Are You There God? It's Me, Margaret by Judy Blume.
The Autobiography of Miss Jane Pittman by Ernest J. Gaines.
Bermuda Triangle by Charles Berlitz.
Black Boy by Richard Wright.
Bless the Beasts and Children by Glendon Swarthout.
Brave New World by Aldous Huxley.
Brideshead Revisited by Evelyn Waugh.
The Call of the Wild by Jack London.
Canterbury Tales by Geoffrey Chaucer.
The Catcher in the Rye by J.D. Salinger.

Cat's Cradle by Kurt Vonnegut, Jr.

Chesapeake by James Michener.

The Chosen by Chaim Potok.

The Contender by Robert Lipsyte.

Crime and Punishment by Fyodor Dostoevski.

The Crucible by Arthur Miller.

Cry, The Beloved Country by Alan Paton.

Cyrano de Bergerac by Edmond Rostand.

Daisy Miller by Henry James.

Daughter of Time by Josephine Tey.

A Death in the Family by James Agee.

Death is a Noun by John Langone.

Death of a Salesman by Arthur Miller.

Anne Frank: The Diary of a Young Girl by Anne Frank.

Don Quixote by Cervantes.

Don't Look and It Won't Hurt by Richard Peck.

A Dove of the East and Other Stories by Mark Helprin

Dune Trilogy by Frank Herbert.

The Effect of Gamma Rays on Man-in-the-Moon Marigolds by Paul Zindel.

A Farewell to Arms by Ernest Hemingway.

Flowers for Algernon by Daniel Keyes.

Foundation Trilogy by Isaac Asimov.

Gone With the Wind by Margaret Mitchell.

The Good Earth by Pearl S. Buck.

The Grapes of Wrath by John Steinbeck.

Great Expectations by Charles Dickens.

The Great Gatsby by F. Scott Fitzgerald.

Hamlet by William Shakespeare.

The Heart is a Lonely Hunter by Carson McCullers.

Henderson the Rain King by Saul Bellow.

Hiroshima by John Hersey.

The Hobbit /The Lord of the Rings Trilogy by J.R.R. Tolkien.

Holocaust by Gerald Green.

House of Seven Gables by Nathaniel Hawthorne

I Am the Cheese by Robert Cormier.

It's Not the End of the World by Judy Blume.

Jane Eyre by Charlotte Bronte.

Joy in the Morning by Betty Smith.

The Late Great Me by Sandra Scoppettone.

Laughing Boy by Oliver LaFarge.

Long Day's Journey into Night by Eugene O'Neill.

Look Homeward Angel by Thomas Wolfe.

Lord of the Flies by William Golding.

Macbeth by William Shakespeare.

Mistress Masham's Repose by T.H. White.

Moby Dick by Herman Melville.

Native Son by Richard Wright.

A Night to Remember by Walter Lord.

1984 by George Orwell.

The Odyssey by Homer.

Of Mice and Men by John Steinbeck.

The Old Man and the Sea by Ernest Hemingway.

One Day in the Life of Ivan Denisovitch by Alexander Solzhenitsyn.

One Flew Over the Cuckoo's Nest by Ken Kesey.

The Once and Future King by T. H. White.

Ordinary People by Judith Guest.

Our Town by Thornton Wilder.

Out of Love by Hilma Wolitzer.

The Outsiders by S. E. Hinton.

Portrait of the Artist as a Young Man by James Joyce.

The Princess Bride by William Goldman.

The Promise by Danielle Steel.

Rebecca by Daphne du Maurier.

The Rise and Fall of the Third Reich by William Shirer.

Romeo and Juliet by William Shakespeare.

Roots by Alex Haley.

A Separate Peace by John Knowles.

Seventeenth Summer by Maureen Daly.

The Shining by Stephen King.

Something Wicked This Way Comes by Ray Bradbury.

A Summer to Die by Lois Lowry.

A Tale of Two Cities by Charles Dickens.

The Thorn Birds by Colleen McCullough.

The Three Musketeers by Alexandre Dumas.

To Kill a Mockingbird by Harper Lee.

A Tree Grows in Brooklyn by Betty Smith.

The Trojan Women by Euripides

2001: A Space Odyssey by Arthur C. Clarke.

Watership Down by Richard Adams.

Where the Red Fern Grows by Wilson Rawls.

Winning by Robin Brancato.

The Wizard of Earthsea by Ursula K. LeGuin.

Wuthering Heights by Emily Bronte.

BIBLIOGRAPHY OF HELPFUL BOOK GUIDES

Need more than a title to help you choose a good book? Here's a list of paperbacks describing all kinds of books that appeal to teenage readers. See if they are on hand in your school or local library.

Most librarians receive a helpful pamphlet published by the American Library Association every year. Ask your librarian for a copy of this booklist, "Best Books for Young Adults."

Carlsen, G. Robert, editor, *Books and the Teenage Reader,* Bantam, 1980.

Cullinan, Bernice, and **M. Jerry Weiss,** editors, *Books I Read When I Was Young,* Avon Books, 1980.

Walker, Jerry L., editor, *Your Reading: A Booklist for Junior High Students,* National Council for Teachers of English, 1975.

Weber, J. Sherwood, editor, *Good Reading,* New American Library, 1980.

Wilson, Jean, editor, *Books for You,* Pocket Books in conjunction with the National Council for Teachers of English, 1971.

White, Marian, editor, *High Interest, Easy Reading for Junior and Senior High School Students,* Scholastic Inc., in conjunction with the National Council of Teachers of English, 1972.

PROOFREADER'S CHECKLIST

a̲̲ (capital letter)   These three lines under a letter indicate that the letter should be capitalized.

/	(lower case or split letters or words)	This mark placed *through* a letter indicates that the letter should be lower case. Placed *between* two letters it indicates that two words should be formed.
$\wedge$	(caret insert)	This mark indicates that a word, phrase, or punctuation mark is being added.
✗	(deletion line)	This mark shows that a word, phrase, or punctuation mark is being taken out.
$\sim$	(letter or word reversal)	This mark shows that two letters or two words should be reversed.
⊂	(connect)	This mark shows that two letters or two words should be joined together.
¶	(paragraph mark)	This mark indicates the need to indent for a new paragraph.
⊙	(period)	This indicates that a period should be added.

GLOSSARY OF LITERARY TERMS

Allegory: a story in which characters symbolize the author's concepts.

Antagonist: a character who opposes the main character or protagonist.

Atmosphere: the mood or feeling of a work; usually associated with the setting.

Autobiography: a biography written about oneself.

Bibliography: a list of writings about a particular author or subject.

Biography: a factual book dealing with a person's life.

Caricature: a character presented with ridiculous exaggeration.

Characterization: method and style in which an author presents and develops a character.

Climax: the crisis, high point, or most intense moment of a novel or play.

Comedy: a light and humorous literary work with a happy ending.

Conflict: the main struggle or tension in a story, novel, or play.

Critique: a criticism or review of a literary work.

Drama: a literary work written for the stage.

Epilogue: an episode or scene that takes place after the end of a story, novel, or play.

Episode: an incident or group of related incidents and happenings in a story, novel, or play.

Essay: a short prose composition dealing with one main idea; usually expresses the personal viewpoint of the author.

Exposition: an explanation of information to help the reader understand the situation at the beginning of a story or novel.

Fable: a short story that reveals some moral message or truth.

Fantasy: an imaginative work containing supernatural elements.

Fiction: an imaginary story, novel, play, or narrative poem.

Flashback: an interruption in the sequence of a work, which goes back to an earlier event.

Figure of speech: an expression that departs from the usual meaning of words in order to create a special effect.

Foil: a character used to contrast with another character.

Foreshadowing: a hint of the eventual outcome of a story.

Genre: a type, kind, or style of writing. Biographies, novels, short stories, plays, poems, essays, etc., are all examples of different genres.

Hero: the principal figure in a work, usually possessing noble, positive qualities.

Ideas: views, attitudes, and feelings presented by an author; aspects of an author's philosophy.

Imagery: sensory descriptions or figures of speech.

Incident: an occurrence, episode, or event in a story.

Irony: a figure of speech in which a word apparently meaning one thing actually implies the opposite.

Legend: an unverifiable popular story from the past.

Melodramatic: an overly romantic, sensational, violent, sentimental, or exaggerated quality in a literary work.

Metaphor: a figure of speech in which a comparison is implied; usually a comparison between two dissimilar things. Example: The fog is a blanket hiding everything within it.

Monologue: a solo speech or narrative.

Mood: the emotional feeling in a literary work.

Motivation: the purpose of a character's behavior.

Myth: a story involving supernatural persons and events; often explains natural or historical events.

Narrative: an account or story of related events.

Narrator: the teller of the story.

Novel: a book-length fictitious narrative.

Novella: a story shorter than a novel but longer than a short story.

Parable: a simple story with an obvious moral.

Paradox: a contradictory statement or situation.

Parody: a composition that humorously imitates a serious work.

Plot: the succession of incidents in a story; the arrangement of those events.

Point of view: the way in which a reader is presented with a story. A story told in the *first person* is related from the position of a character who uses the "I" voice. A story told in the *third person* is related by an all-knowing narrator who describes events and characters from the outside.

Prologue: an event that takes place before the formal beginning of a work.

Protagonist: the main character, who receives most of the author's attention.

Purpose: the author's aim, goal, or intention within a literary work.

Resolution: the outcome of a crisis or conflict in a literary work.

Romantic: fanciful, extravagant, or exaggerated view of life in a literary work.

Satire: ridicule of human foibles, follies, and weaknesses.

Sentimentality: fanciful or exaggerated feelings of an overly tender type.

Setting: the time, place, and circumstances in a literary work.

Stock character: a recognizable or stereotyped character who has been overused in literature.

Style: an author's manner of expression.

Subplot: a secondary plot that is woven into the main plot.

Symbol: a character, event, or object that stands for an idea.

Theme: the underlying idea in a literary work.

Thesis: a specific idea or point that the author intends to prove in a literary work.

Tone: the general mood, spirit, feeling, or quality of a literary work.

Tragedy: a serious play in which the hero is overcome by obstacles that he attempts to surmount.

Villain: a treacherous or wicked opponent of the hero.

FILE CARD FORM

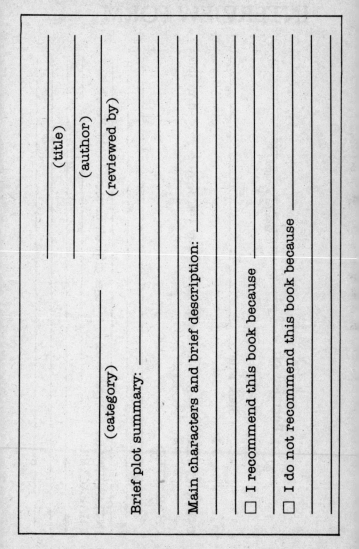

(title)

(author)

(reviewed by)

(category)

Brief plot summary:

Main characters and brief description:

☐ I recommend this book because

☐ I do not recommend this book because

CHARACTER INTERVIEW FORM

Interview of: _____ (character's name)

Book title: _____

INTERVIEWER: How you feel about the way you were portrayed in this book?

CHARACTER: _____
_____
_____

INTERVIEWER: What was your most difficult moment in the book?

CHARACTER: _____
_____
_____
_____

INTERVIEWER: What was going through your mind during this difficult moment? _____

CHARACTER: _____
_____
_____

INTERVIEWER: If you could change any of your actions in the book, what would you do differently? _____

CHARACTER: _____
_____
_____

INTERVIEWER: How did you really feel about the other main characters in the book? _____

CHARACTER: _____
_____
_____

INTERVIEWER: Describe your strengths and weaknesses to the reader.

CHARACTER: _____

_____

_____

INTERVIEWER: Would you like the reader to know other things about you that were not covered in the book? If so, describe these characteristics.

CHARACTER: _____

_____

_____

INTERVIEWER: What are your feelings about the way your author ended the book?

CHARACTER: _____

_____

_____

_____

READING RECORD SHEET

TITLE	AUTHOR	DATE READ	BOOK REPORT GRADE	RATING (Great, Good, Fair, Not Recommended)	COMMENTS

INDEX